THE
ENCYCLOPEDIA
—— OF OUR ——
awesome
EARTH

© Aladdin Books Ltd 1999
Produced by
Aladdin Books Ltd
28 Percy Street
London W1P 0LD

First published in the United States in 1999 by
Copper Beech Books,
an imprint of
The Millbrook Press
2 Old New Milford Road
Brookfield, Connecticut 06804

Concept, editorial, and design by
David West Children's Books

Designer: Flick Killerby

Editor: Liz White

Library of Congress Cataloging-in-Publication Data
The encyclopedia of our awesome earth.
p. cm.
Includes index.
Summary: Provides information about geological and weather
phenomena such as tornadoes, earthquakes, volcanoes, tidal waves,
thunder clouds, blizzards, and weather prediction.
ISBN 0-7613-0831-8
1. Earth sciences Miscellanea Juvenile literature.
[1. Earth sciences Miscellanea.]
QE29.E53 1999   99-39169
550–dc21   CIP
Printed in Belgium

5 4 3

THE
ENCYCLOPEDIA
—OF OUR—
awesome
EARTH

COPPER BEECH BOOKS
BROOKFIELD, CONNECTICUT

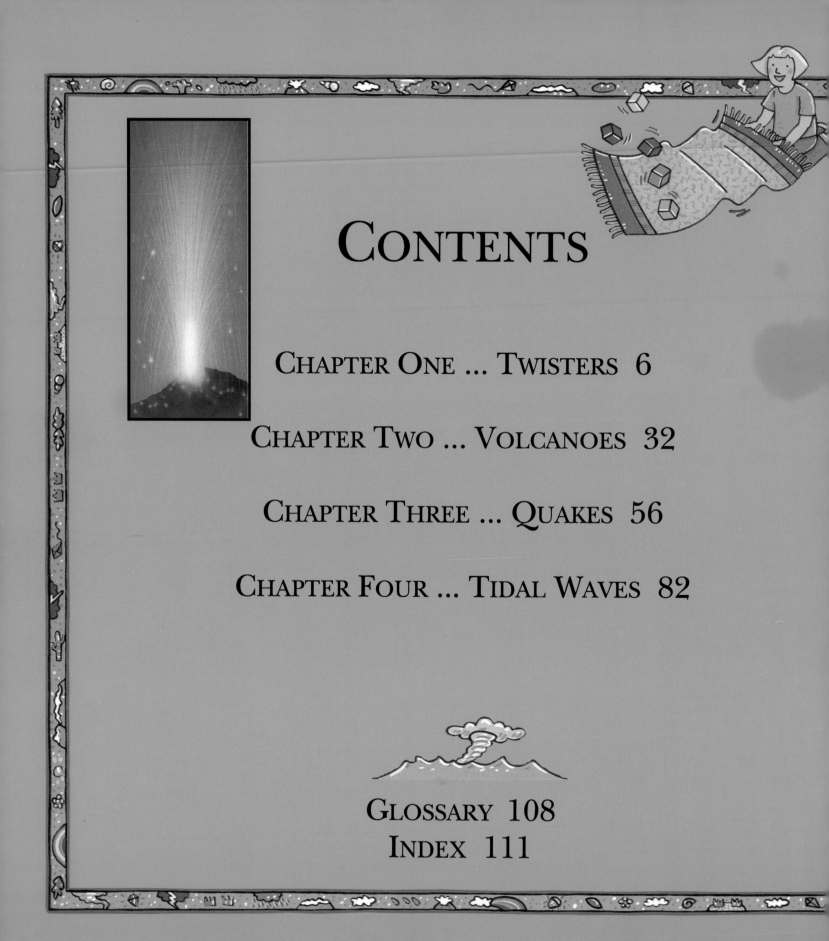

CONTENTS

Introduction

Discover for yourself the most amazing facts about our awesome world from volcanic eruptions, to earthquakes, twisters, and tidal waves ravaging the earth.

Chapter by chapter this book will keep you informed about the natural phenomena of the world around you; from rivers of lava, and volcanoes in space, to thunderclouds, typhoons, hurricanes, sandstorms, tidal waves, waterspouts, and flooding. Learn about the plates that cover the earth, volcanic ash, hailstones, blizzards, tornadoes, and weather prediction. With all these topics to read about, the *Encyclopedia of our Awesome Earth* introduces you to the amazing world in which you live.

Look for this symbol that means there is a fun project for you to try.

Is it true or is it false? Watch for this symbol and try to answer the question before reading on for the answer.

Don't forget to check the borders for extra amazing facts.

Chapter One

twisters

By Kate Petty

Illustrated by
Peter Roberts
and Jo Moore

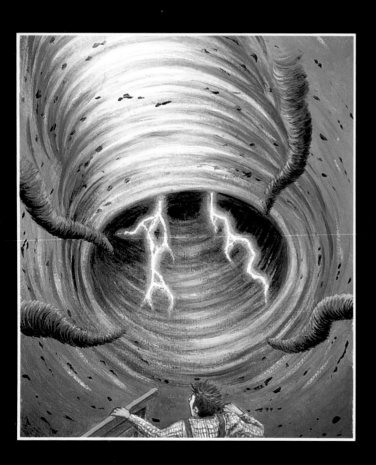

Introduction

Discover for yourself the most amazing facts about violent weather, from the hailstone that was as big as a tennis ball (but much heavier!) to the storm surge that can fling boats half a mile inland.

Did you know that you can float up and down in clouds? ... that thunderheads can be over nine miles high? ... that thunder is the sound of lightning? ... that people lie down in a blizzard? ... that a monsoon can last up to six months? ... that dust devils can be half a mile high? ... that it can rain frogs, fish, and schoolchildren? ... that hurricanes can pile up boats like bath toys?

I didn't know that

you can float up and down in clouds. William Rankin did when he bailed out of his plane in a violent thunderstorm. He was bounced around in the clouds, battered by the wind, for a terrifying 40 minutes before finally parachuting to safety.

In 1876, Denonath Sircar of Bangladesh clung to a broken branch all night to save himself in a flood that washed away millions of homes.

The terrible hurricane that hit the Caribbean in 1780 killed 20,000 people. The wind was so violent that it hurled a 12-pound cannon 420 feet.

In 1931, a Minnesota tornado tossed a railroad car 82 feet through the air.

Deanna Wyant and her boyfriend actually flew around the room when a tornado hit their apartment in 1965. The building collapsed but miraculously they both survived!

I didn't know that

thunderheads can be over nine miles high. The name for a thundercloud is cumulonimbus. Cumulus means "heaped" and nimbus means "rain cloud." You can see fluffy, low-level cumulus clouds building up into tall thunderclouds in warm weather.

Leave an upturned jar on a saucer of water in a sunny spot for an hour. The heat of the sun will cause some of the water to *evaporate* and rise as invisible water vapor. Watch the *condensation* forming on the glass as the invisible water vapor cools and it starts to "rain."

Cold, dry air

Warm, wet air

Clouds can be formed in many ways. In this case, a warm air mass moves in from the right. It rises over cold air moving in from the left. Rain forms where the masses meet.

3 The base of the cloud is low. The top is very high.

2 The air cools as it gets higher and droplets form.

1 In hot weather warm, wet air and dust rise to form cumulus clouds.

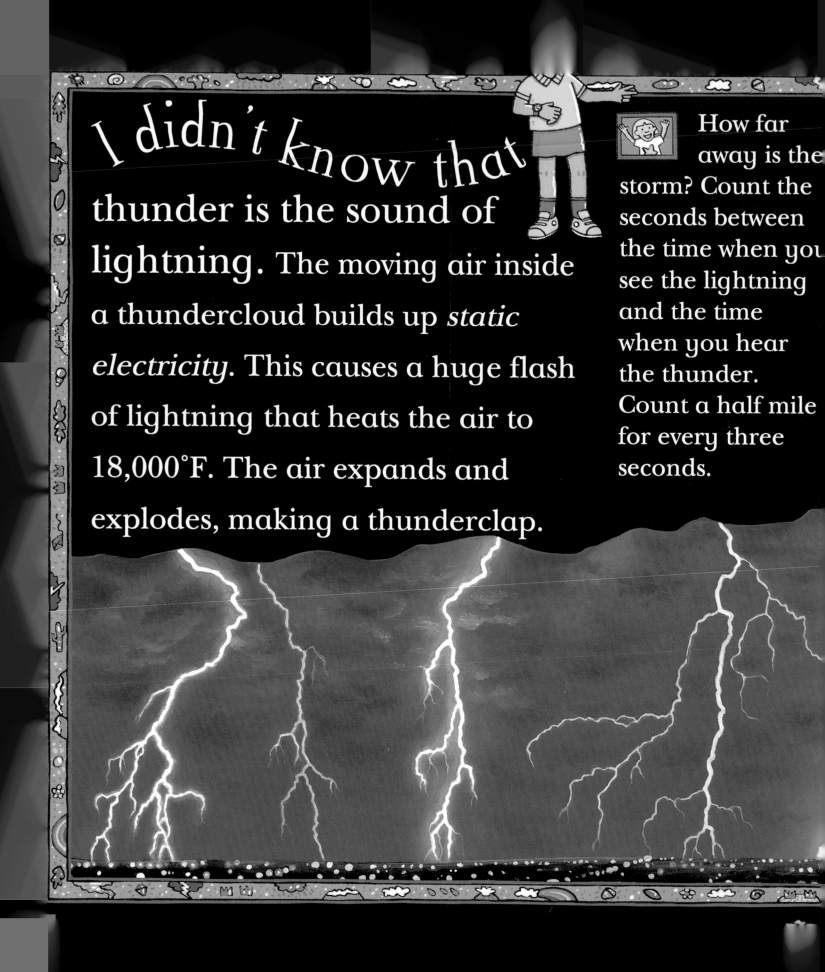

I didn't know that

thunder is the sound of lightning. The moving air inside a thundercloud builds up *static electricity*. This causes a huge flash of lightning that heats the air to 18,000°F. The air expands and explodes, making a thunderclap.

How far away is the storm? Count the seconds between the time when you see the lightning and the time when you hear the thunder. Count a half mile for every three seconds.

Don't try Benjamin Franklin's famous 1752 experiment with a kite and a key to prove the electrical nature of lightning. A Swedish scientist, trying it out for himself in 1909, was electrocuted.

Reports of "ball lightning" have not been scientifically proved. A ball of lightning supposedly floated around a hotel room in France before drifting out of the window and exploding nearby.

In 1894, a hailstone that landed in the U.S. contained a frozen turtle.

True or false?

Firing shells at clouds can prevent hailstorms.

Answer: **True**

Anti-hail gunners in Uzbekistan fire shells, scattering tiny particles into the clouds. The smaller hailstones that cling to them melt before reaching the ground.

The largest hailstones fell during a storm in Bangladesh that killed 92 people in 1986. Each hailstone weighed up to two pounds.

I didn't know that some hailstones are the size of tennis balls. In India, these huge hailstones smashed car windshields, flattened crops, and killed thousands of birds. Many farmers now insure themselves against hail damage.

SEARCH & FIND
Can you find the fish?

A hailstone has layers, like an onion. It picks up a layer of ice each time it goes up and down in a thundercloud.

I didn't know that

people lie down in a blizzard. This is a good survival tip as the blanket of snow traps a layer of warm air around the body. Remember to make an airhole! Animals often survive in the snow this way.

SEARCH & FIND
Can you find the backpack?
FIND SEARCH &

Snowflakes form when water vapor rapidly freezes as crystals around dust particles. Each snow crystal has six sides and each one is unique. Catch some on a dark glove and study them (quickly!) through a magnifying glass.

In 1978, 27 inches of snow fell on Boston in 24 hours.

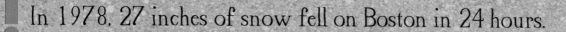

Avalanche! A weakness in a layer of snow on a slope or a precipice can start an avalanche. As thousands of tons of snow roars downhill, it can reach speeds of over 186 mph, burying everything in its path.

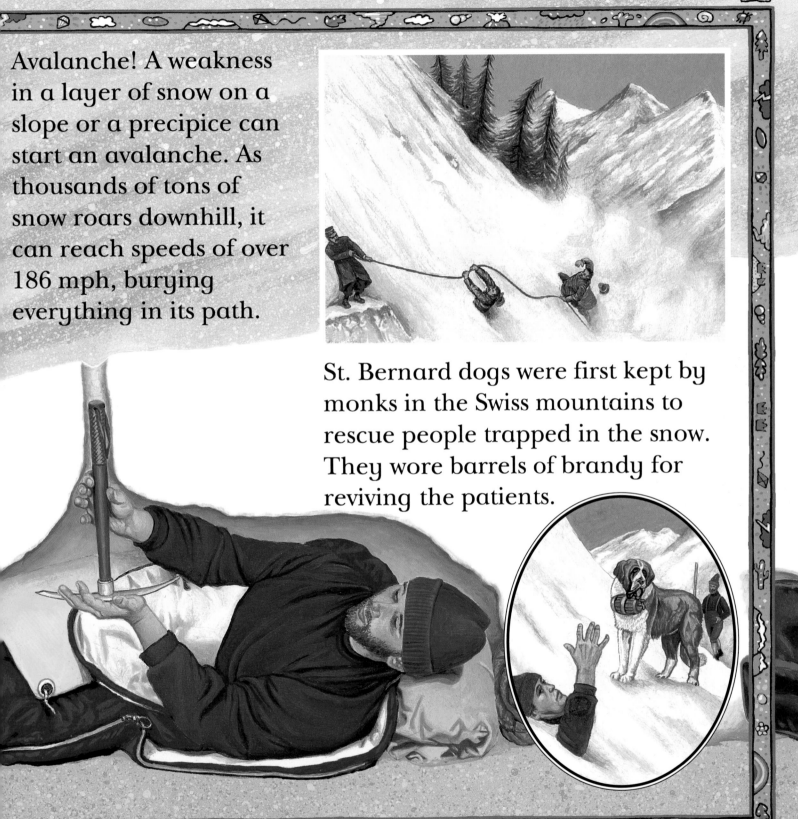

St. Bernard dogs were first kept by monks in the Swiss mountains to rescue people trapped in the snow. They wore barrels of brandy for reviving the patients.

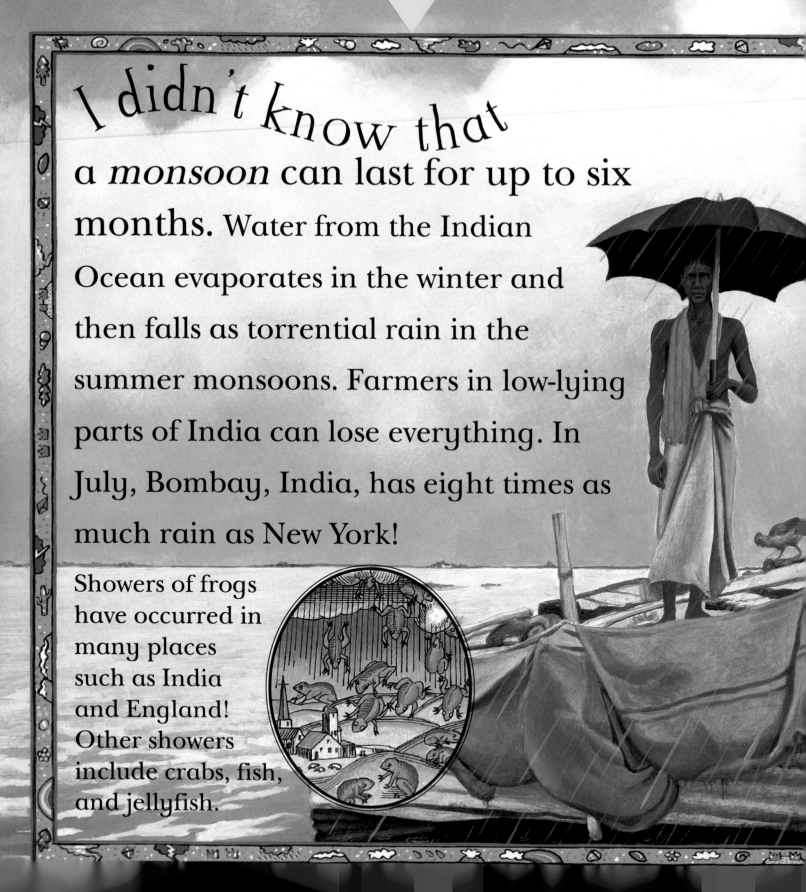

I didn't know that

a *monsoon* can last for up to six months. Water from the Indian Ocean evaporates in the winter and then falls as torrential rain in the summer monsoons. Farmers in low-lying parts of India can lose everything. In July, Bombay, India, has eight times as much rain as New York!

Showers of frogs have occurred in many places such as India and England! Other showers include crabs, fish, and jellyfish.

Land is flooded when rain makes a river rise over its banks. Noah's flood is based on fact. There were floods in the Tigris-Euphrates valley in Turkey and Mesopotamia around 4000 B.C.

You can make your own rain gauge from a flat-bottomed plastic bottle. Find out how much rain falls in July where you live.

Top of plastic bottle is cut and placed upside down

Measure in inches

Bottom filled with water to point where measure starts

I didn't know that

hurricanes have eyes. In a hurricane the air moves around, spiraling upward to form a rotating circle of wind around a central "chimney." This calm center is called the "eye."

Can you find the satellite?

Eye

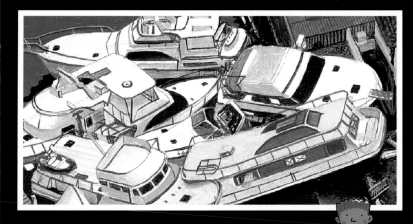

Winds over 186 mph can cause unimaginable destruction. In 1992, Hurricane Andrew hit an area south of Florida, tearing roofs and walls off houses, smashing trees and cars, and piling up boats like little plastic toys!

 True or false?

Hurricanes are given girls' and boys' names.

Answer: **True**

Atlantic hurricanes are given alternate girls' and boys' names in alphabetical order from the beginning of the season. This makes them easier to identify.

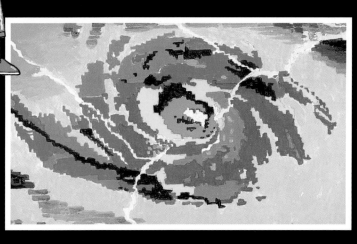

Infra-red pictures from satellites provide color-coded information about *tropical storms.* Scientists can track their progress and warn people in time.

Hurricane Andrew caused $46.5 billion worth of damage.

Even a warship such as an aircraft carrier can crumple like tin in a typhoon. This is what happened to *U.S.S. Hornet* near Okinawa, Japan, in 1945.

I didn't know that

typhoons can sink ships. Tropical storms can whip up mountainous waves. The highest wave ever measured was 85 feet, but the highest ever seen was 111 feet. Ships are helpless in such stormy seas.

True or false?
Hurricanes, tropical cyclones, and typhoons are all the same thing.

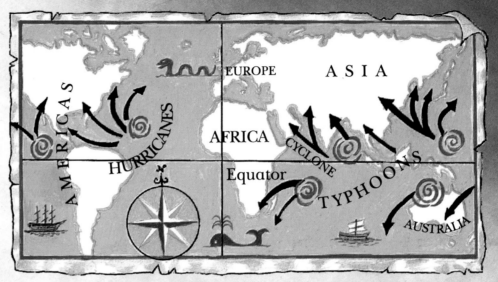

Answer: **True**
Tropical storms are called hurricanes in the Atlantic Ocean, cyclones in the Indian Ocean, typhoons in the China Sea, and willy-willies in Australia.

A *storm surge* carried this boat nearly a half mile inland. Huge waves can surge in ahead of a hurricane, flooding low-lying areas.

I didn't know that

tornadoes can make children fly.

Tornadoes are like small, ferocious storms. People, animals, and whole houses can be picked up and dropped some distance away. In 1986, thirteen Chinese schoolchildren were carried 12 miles by a tornado before being deposited completely unharmed!

A dust devil in the desert is a miniature tornado. Spinning winds whirl sand and dust to heights of between 300–3,000 feet.

A whirling cloud turns into a waterspout as water is sucked up. It is spectacular, but not terribly dangerous.

SEARCH & FIND

Can you find 13 children?

A tornado, or "twister," comes down out of thunder-clouds like an "elephant's trunk," a spinning funnel of cloud that sucks up dust and soil. The funnel gets tighter and the wind gets faster, up to 500 mph.

Some tornadoes are born in hurricanes.

I didn't know that

people chase twisters. The more people understand about tornadoes, the easier it will be to predict when one is coming along. Scientists study tornadoes by following them and putting monitoring equipment in their path to assess their strength.

Tornadoes sometimes appear in pairs. These pairs are called "sisters."

An eyewitness described a tornado in 1928: "The great shaggy end of the funnel hung directly overhead. There was a strong gassy odor. The walls were of rotating clouds with constant flashes of lightning that zigzagged from side to side."

True or false?

People can make their own twisters.

Answer: **True**

But not full-size ones! Japanese scientist Tetsuya Fujita studies miniature tornadoes made of dry ice.

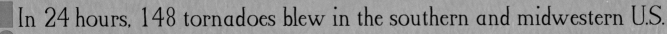
In 24 hours, 148 tornadoes blew in the southern and midwestern U.S.

I didn't know that

sandstorms can strip paint off a car. Loose dust and sand in deserts can easily be whipped up by the wind, flinging millions of stinging grains at every surface. Sand-carrying winds carve desert rocks into strange shapes.

Industrial sandblasting is used to strip dirt and paint off old buildings to make them look new again.

Sand-carved rock found in the desert

A terrifying 9,000-foot-high storm turns the sky dark and sandblasts everything in its path.

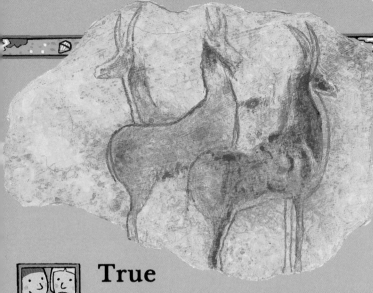

There were dust storms in the American midwest in the 1930s. The rain failed and wind blew the dry soil around. Farmers couldn't grow anything, so people starved.

True or false?

The Sahara has always been a desert.

Answer: **False**

Climate can change. Cave paintings in the Sahara show that it was once home to all types of animals that could only live where there was water and grass.

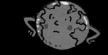

I didn't know that

weather forecasters use information from space. Satellites high above the earth send back pictures of cloud movements. They show where storms are brewing.

This scientist fires a rocket into thunder-clouds. Wires attached to the rocket trigger a charge of lightning.

Weather balloons, called radiosondes, can record and transmit weather conditions as they travel upward.

Weather stations all over the world take temperature, wind, rain, and *air pressure* readings and feed them into computers.

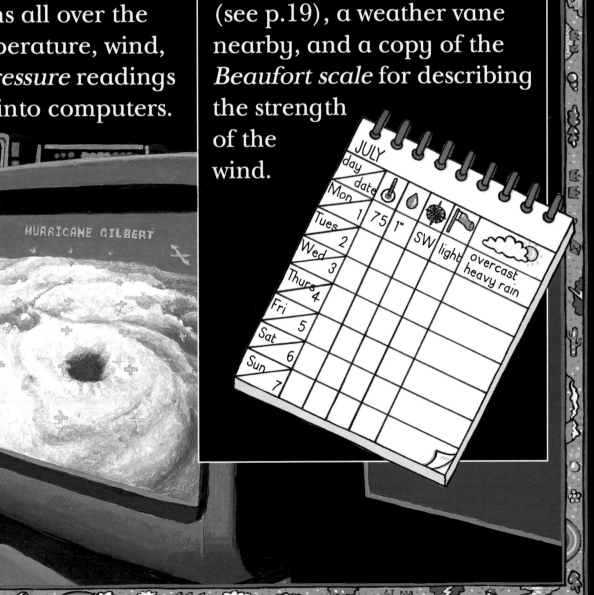

HURRICANE GILBERT

Be a weather observer yourself. Record your observations at the same time every day. You will need a thermometer, a rain gauge (see p.19), a weather vane nearby, and a copy of the *Beaufort scale* for describing the strength of the wind.

JULY
day
date

Mon	1	75	1"			
Tues	2			SW	light	overcast heavy rain
Wed	3					
Thurs	4					
Fri	5					
Sat	6					
Sun	7					

Meteorology comes from Greek and means "thing in the heaven above."

Chapter Two
volcanoes

By Clare Oliver

Illustrated by
Ian Thompson,
Peter Roberts,
and Jo Moore

Introduction

Discover for yourself amazing facts about the earth's volcanoes and the people who study them. Learn about tsunamis, hot springs, black smokers, and about the volcanoes of the past – and in space.

Did you know that the earth is covered in plates? ... that the earth is full of holes? ... that there are rivers of rock? ... that mountains spit ash? ... that ash can freeze people in time? ... that volcanoes make islands? ... that there are chimneys under the sea? ... that you can take a bath in mud?

Copy the map of the earth below, or blow it up on a photocopier. Color it in, then cut along the *fault lines*. Can you fit all the *plates* back together? Can you find the Pacific Ocean plate? There are so many volcanoes around this plate that the area is called the Ring of Fire.

Most earthquakes are not even noticeable, but about every three years there is a violent one somewhere in the world. In 1970, an earthquake in Peru made roads crack and buildings collapse. It caused a massive landslide – and 66,000 deaths.

34

The San Andreas Fault in California is where two plates are sliding past each other in opposite directions. There have been lots of big earthquakes along this line. Even so, many people make their homes there.

I didn't know that

the earth is covered in plates. The earth's *crust* is made of pieces called plates. These don't join neatly – some overlap, and there are gaps between others. Volcanoes and earthquakes usually happen at fault lines where the edges of plates move apart or grate together.

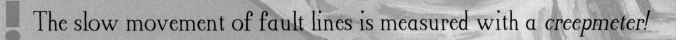

The slow movement of fault lines is measured with a *creepmeter!*

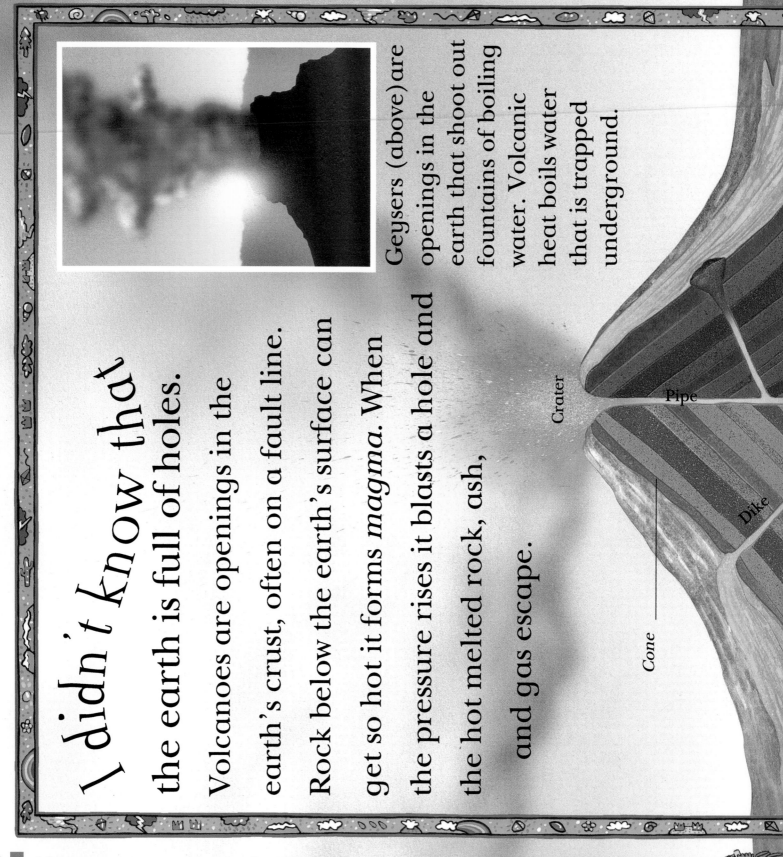

I didn't know that

the earth is full of holes.

Volcanoes are openings in the earth's crust, often on a fault line. Rock below the earth's surface can get so hot it forms *magma*. When the pressure rises it blasts a hole and the hot melted rock, ash, and gas escape.

Geysers (above) are openings in the earth that shoot out fountains of boiling water. Volcanic heat boils water that is trapped underground.

Crater

Pipe

Dike

Cone

Volcanoes are named after Vulcan, Roman god of fire and metalworking.

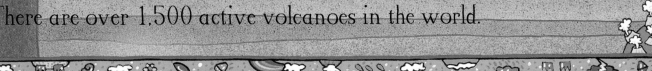

True or false?
There is fire at the center of the earth.

Outer core (liquid metal)

Inner core (solid metal)

Outer mantle (hot rock)

Inner mantle (hot rock)

Answer: **False**
Long ago people believed that a fire inside our planet gave all volcanoes their fiery power. Now we know the earth's core is metal and that a hot *mantle* of rock surrounds the core.

Vent

Magma chamber

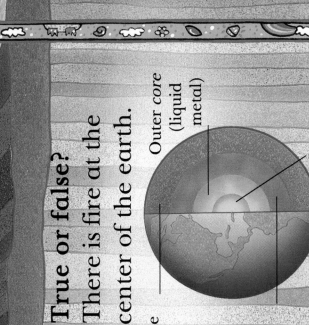

When they *erupt,* volcanoes really blow their top! They leave a *crater.* If it is very big, it's called a *caldera.* The one above is on the Japanese volcano, Shirane. It's been so long since Shirane erupted that its crater has filled with rainwater and become a lake.

37

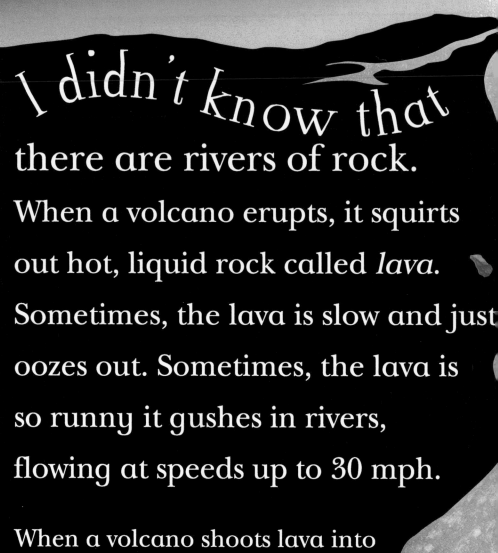

I didn't know that

there are rivers of rock.

When a volcano erupts, it squirts out hot, liquid rock called *lava*. Sometimes, the lava is slow and just oozes out. Sometimes, the lava is so runny it gushes in rivers, flowing at speeds up to 30 mph.

When a volcano shoots lava into the air it makes a fountain of fire that can reach 300 ft in height. Molten rock can also come out as house-sized lava bombs, little stones called lapilli, or clouds of ash and dust.

True or false?
Lava has skin.

SEARCH & FIND
Can you find five lava bombs?
FIND & SEARCH

Answer: **True**
Pahoehoe (pa hoy hoy) is a very hot, fluid type of lava that grows a smooth skin on top as it cools. The hot flow continues underneath, even though the crust may be hard enough to walk across.

Warning – adult help needed!
Make an eruption! Half fill a jar with baking soda. Cut a circle out of cardboard. Make a slit to the middle and tape into a cone shape. Cut a hole at the top of the cone and place over the jar. Add some red food coloring to vinegar. Pour it into the jar, then stand back! This can be messy. Wear old clothes and do it outdoors!

True or false?
There really is a blue moon.

Answer: **True**

Floating clouds of volcanic ash do strange things to light. They can even make the moon and sun seem to glow blue or green!

 The static in an ash cloud can also make lightning. To make static put a metal tray on a plastic bag. Attach a clay "handle" to the tray, then rub it around on the bag. Lift the tray and, with your other hand, touch its edge with a metal fork to see sparks fly!

Mount St. Helens is 4,500 years old - young for a volcano.

I didn't know that

mountains spit ash. The most violent volcanoes blast out ash and gas. The force of Mount St. Helens' eruption in 1980 was as powerful as 500 atomic bombs going off. The cloud gave amazing red sunsets and ash fell over 700 miles away in Colorado.

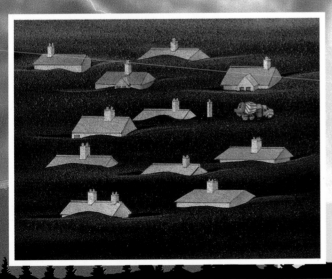

Ash clouds can block out the sun for days. In 1973, the cloud from an eruption on Heimaey (left), off Iceland, left behind a thick blanket of black ash. In some places the ash was over 19 ft deep.

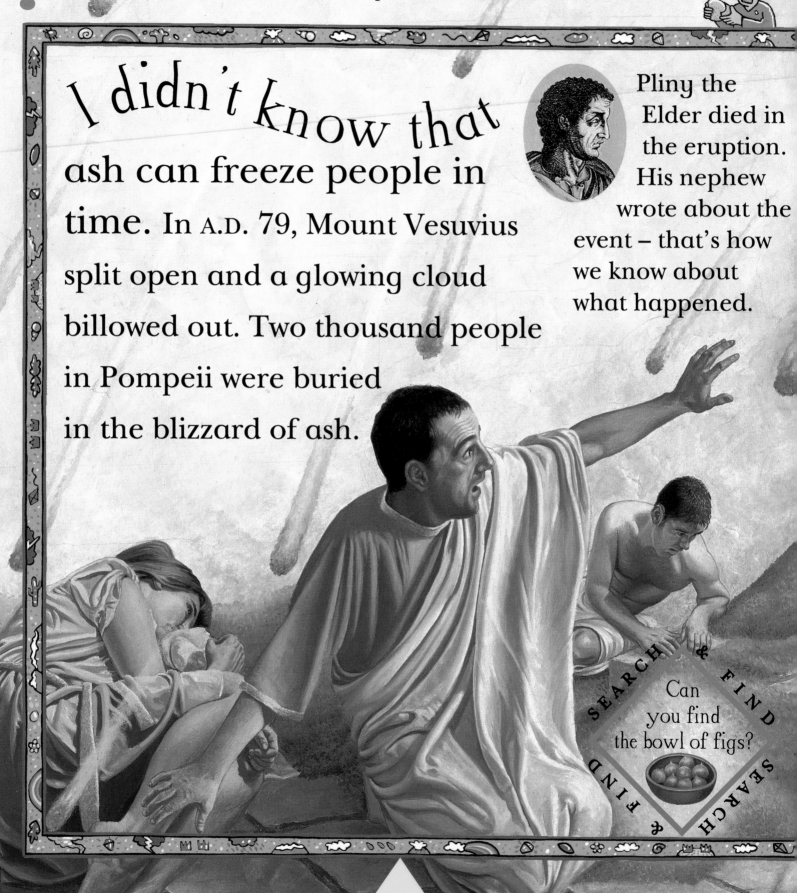

I didn't know that

ash can freeze people in time. In A.D. 79, Mount Vesuvius split open and a glowing cloud billowed out. Two thousand people in Pompeii were buried in the blizzard of ash.

Pliny the Elder died in the eruption. His nephew wrote about the event – that's how we know about what happened.

SEARCH & FIND
Can you find the bowl of figs?
FIND & SEARCH

Pompeii lay forgotten for 1,600 years. Another eruption uncovered the original town. The bodies had decayed leaving people-shaped holes in the hardened ash. By filling these molds with plaster of Paris, archaeologists made models of the Romans – and their pets!

SEARCH & FIND

Can you find three fulmars?

FIND & SEARCH

Iceland is a land of fire and ice, with several active volcanoes and geysers. It formed over millions of years from volcanic eruptions in the Mid-Oceanic Ridge. It is over 50,000 times bigger than Surtsey.

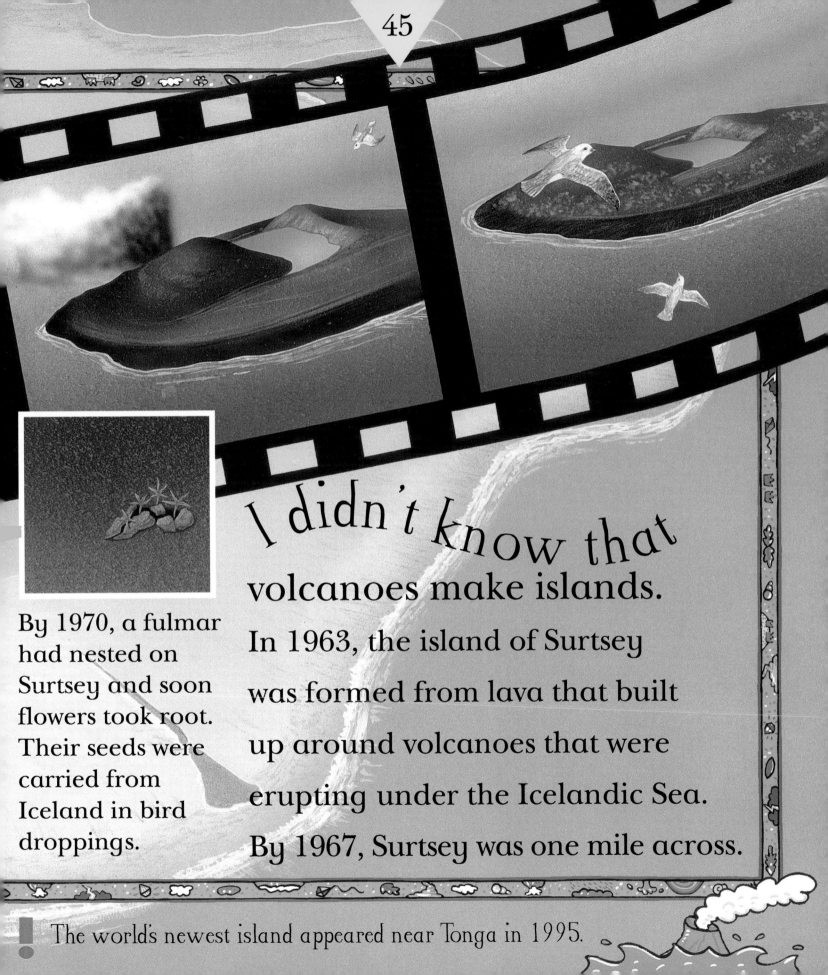

I didn't know that

volcanoes make islands.

In 1963, the island of Surtsey was formed from lava that built up around volcanoes that were erupting under the Icelandic Sea. By 1967, Surtsey was one mile across.

By 1970, a fulmar had nested on Surtsey and soon flowers took root. Their seeds were carried from Iceland in bird droppings.

The world's newest island appeared near Tonga in 1995.

I didn't know that

there are chimneys under the sea. *Black smokers* are formed when hot springs on the seabed gush out water that is black with metals. The metals harden in the cold water, forming tall chimneys.

The world's longest mountain range is the Mid-Oceanic Ridge, a string of volcanoes underwater. Submersibles such as *Alvin* go down and photograph it.

Alvin

47

True or false?

There are pillows on the seabed.

Answer: **True**

Underwater volcanoes erupt slowly because of the weight of the water. Their lava cools to form lumps called pillows.

Swarms of shrimp feed around the chimneys on the water. Spots on their backs can detect the glow given out by the black smokers.

The black smokers leak out poisonous sulfur. Even so, giant tube worms (left) live in the pitch-black water around them, feeding on the sulfur-rich bacteria there.

Most of the earth's volcanoes are under the sea.

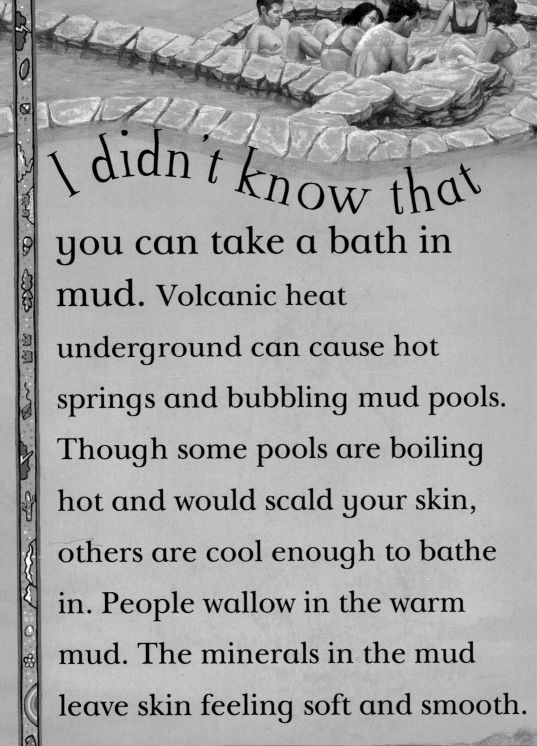

I didn't know that

you can take a bath in mud. Volcanic heat underground can cause hot springs and bubbling mud pools. Though some pools are boiling hot and would scald your skin, others are cool enough to bathe in. People wallow in the warm mud. The minerals in the mud leave skin feeling soft and smooth.

The Japanese town of Beppu has 4,000 hot springs all to itself. The Jungle Bath (above), at over 64,000 sq ft, is the biggest spa in the world.

The Romans believed that spas had healing powers.

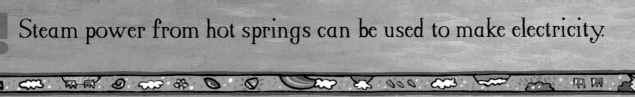

 True or false?
Volcanoes have healing powers.

Answer: **True**
It can't be proven for sure, but lots of people believe they do! In Japan, people like to get up to their necks in warm volcanic sand (left). They believe it can cure illnesses. Drinking the mineral-rich water from hot springs is thought to keep the body healthy and bathing in hot springs soothes pain.

SEARCH & FIND
Can you find the swimming cap?
FIND & SEARCH

I didn't know that

volcanoes fall asleep for centuries. Between eruptions, volcanoes sleep, or are *dormant*. In the Auvergne region of France are remains of *extinct* volcanoes. The cone is weathered away but the hard vent is left. It is hard to be sure that a volcano is really extinct.

Nogorongoro, an extinct volcano in Tanzania (right), is home to flamingos and hippos. Its crater is a lake and the lush grassland around it feeds rhinos and zebras.

 True or false?
Volcanoes make money.

Answer: **True**
They provide us with precious and useful minerals that formed millions of years ago in the hardening lava. This South African diamond mine (right) at Kimberley is on the site of an extinct volcano.

Two volcanoes that erupted in Turkey eight million years ago have long disappeared. But the lava left behind a "city" of fairytale cones, into which people dug houses and churches that can still be seen today.

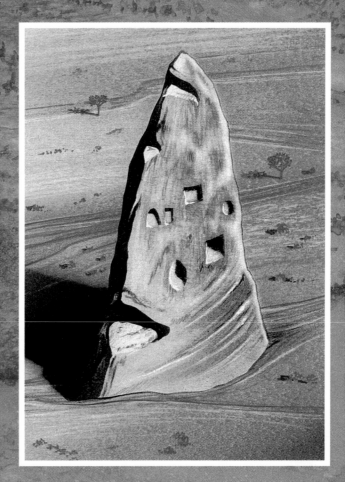

Volcano remains at Le Puy, France

To keep volcanoes dormant, the Aztecs fed them women.

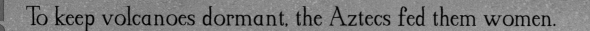

True or false?

The largest volcano is in space.

I didn't know that

there are volcanoes in space. One of Jupiter's moons, Io, is covered in erupting volcanoes. The two *Voyager* spacecraft sent back photographs of the volcanic gas clouds there – which were higher than 30 Mount Everests!

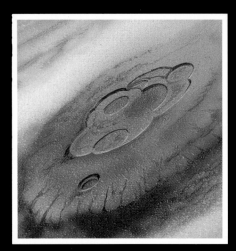

Answer: **True**

The largest known volcano isn't on Earth at all! Mars is home to Olympus Mons, which is 300 miles across and 16 miles high. Like all Mars' volcanoes, Olympus Mons is extinct.

Closer to home, there are volcanoes on our moon, and on Mars and Venus. The *Magellan* spacecraft used radar to take pictures of Venus' volcanoes.

Most craters we see on planets are from *meteorites*, not volcanoes.

Voyager

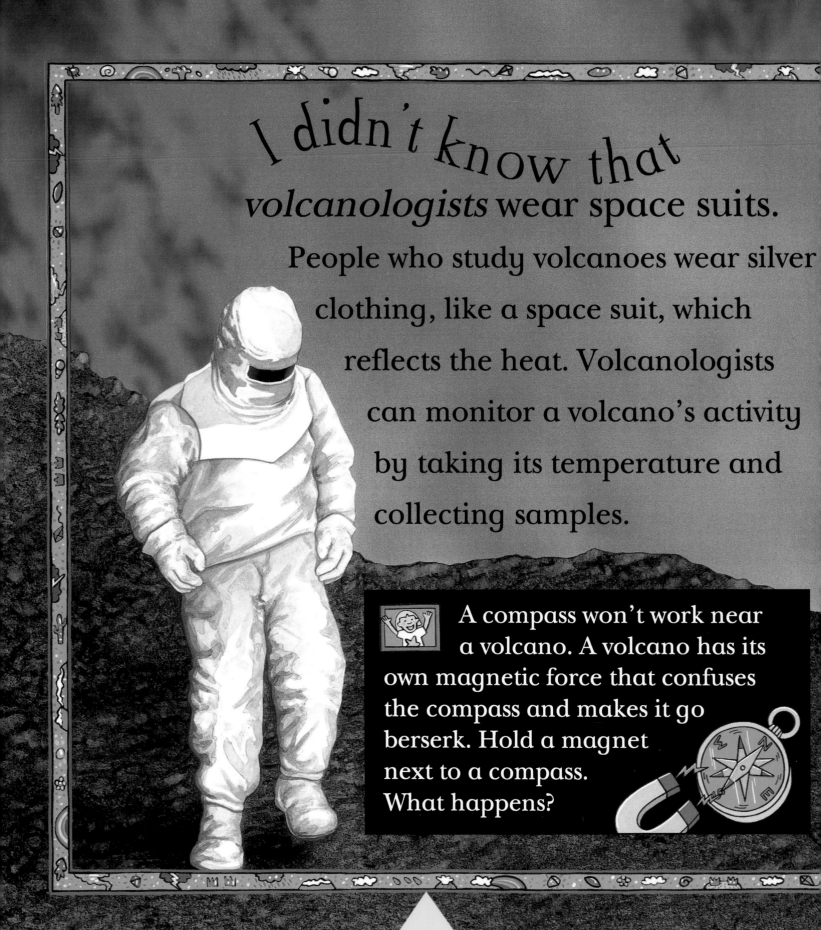

I didn't know that

volcanologists wear space suits.
People who study volcanoes wear silver
clothing, like a space suit, which
reflects the heat. Volcanologists
can monitor a volcano's activity
by taking its temperature and
collecting samples.

A compass won't work near
a volcano. A volcano has its
own magnetic force that confuses
the compass and makes it go
berserk. Hold a magnet
next to a compass.
What happens?

In areas where there are lots of volcanoes, people have to prepare for emergencies. This is a lava bomb shelter in Sakurajima, Japan. Inside, people are safe from the showers of lava bombs.

Volcanologists take samples of lava to examine in the laboratory. They swirl a long pole into the flow to collect it – just like cotton candy collects around its wooden stick.

Volcanologists wear gas masks so they don't breathe in poisonous gases, or choke on ash. Finding out about volcanoes is a dangerous job. When volcanologists can forecast eruptions, they can save lives.

Chapter Three

quakes

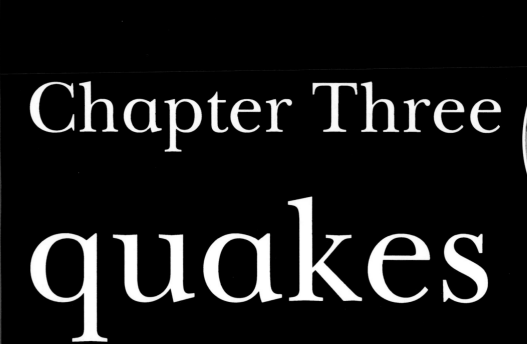

By Clare Oliver

Illustrated by Peter Roberts, Jo Moore, and Graham Kennedy

Introduction

Discover for yourself the most amazing facts about earthquakes and the devastation they can cause. Learn how to predict them, and find out what to do if you are caught in one.

Did you know that quakes split the ground open? ... that waves travel through land? ... that dragons and toads sense quakes? ... that quakes topple bridges? ... that a table can save your life? ... that you can drown in mud? ... that dogs rescue quake victims? ... that pyramid-shaped buildings are very strong?

The longest-ever recorded quake lasted four minutes in Alaska in 1964. The ocean bed was shaken up and down, causing a 30-foot-high wall of water to hit the coast.

I didn't know that quakes split the ground open. The ground beneath your feet may feel firm, but it's not! Sometimes strains build up under the surface, the ground rumbles, and the solid rock cracks apart. This is called a tremor or, if it's big, an earthquake.

A big quake struck Afghanistan in 1998. Many people's remote homes were destroyed so they had to resettle elsewhere.

True or false?
An earthquake at night is called a moonquake.

Answer: **False**
A moonquake is a tremor on the moon. Sometimes pieces of space rock, called meteorites, smash into the moon and make the ground shake.

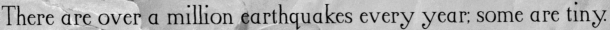
There are over a million earthquakes every year; some are tiny.

I didn't know that

waves travel through land.

The earth's surface is covered in plates that constantly push against each other. When the plates move apart, shock waves are sent through the land. You can't see shock waves but you can feel them.

Most earthquakes happen along fault lines where the rocks are weak and where two or more plates meet.

SEARCH & FIND
Can you find four cars?
FIND & SEARCH

The shock waves start deep underground, at the *focus* of the pressure between the plates. The place where these waves hit the surface will be the earthquake's center, which scientists call the *epicenter*.

Epicenter

Fault

Focus

Plates start to move.

Quake occurs.

The pressure can build up for centuries, but eventually — snap! — the plates shift. The pressure escapes in the form of shock waves that ripple outward from the quake's focus.

See what happens when one of the earth's plates shifts. For the earth's plate, use a rug. Add some buildings: small boxes will do. Pull one end of the rug sharply to move the "plate." What happens to the boxes?

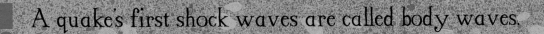

A quake's first shock waves are called body waves.

On the San Andreas Fault, in California, beams of laser light shine across the fault. If a section of earth slips a tiny bit, detectors on the other side measure the slippage.

I didn't know that

dragons and toads sense quakes. This bronze pot (right) was the first quake detector. In a tremor, a dragon would drop its ball into a toad's mouth. By seeing which toad held a ball, the inventor knew where the quake was starting.

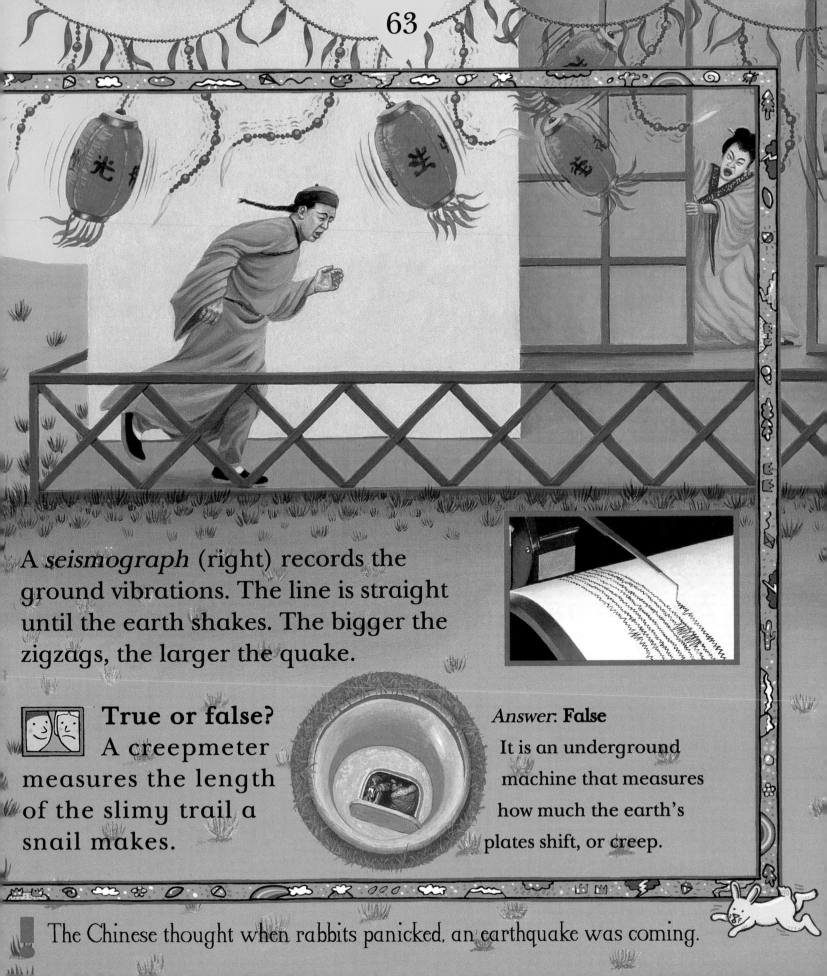

A *seismograph* (right) records the ground vibrations. The line is straight until the earth shakes. The bigger the zigzags, the larger the quake.

True or false?
A creepmeter measures the length of the slimy trail a snail makes.

Answer: **False**
It is an underground machine that measures how much the earth's plates shift, or creep.

The Chinese thought when rabbits panicked, an earthquake was coming.

I didn't know that

earthquakes ring bells.

Scientists number earthquakes to show their strength. The Richter scale grades the strength of an earthquake from 0-9 using seismograph readings. A quake that makes a church bell ring is grade 4 on the Richter scale.

The *Mercalli scale* (right) grades quakes from I (one) to XII (twelve). A grade IV (four) quake causes the same sort of shaking as a heavy truck passing.

1. EARTHQUAKE FELT BY INSTRUMENTS AND ONLY A FEW PEOPLE.

4. FELT INDOORS LIKE PASSING OF HEAVY TRUCKS. DISHES AND WINDOWS RATTLE.

7. FELT BY DRIVERS. WAVES ON PONDS. DIFFICULT TO STAND.

8. CHIMNEYS AND MONUMENTS COLLAPSE.

11. FEW BUILDINGS LEFT STANDING. BRIDGES AND UNDERGROUND PIPES DESTROYED. CRACKS IN THE GROUND.

Mercalli based his scale on what quake victims reported.

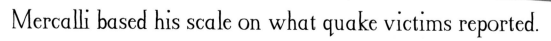

2 FELT ON UPPER FLOORS BY PEOPLE RESTING.

3. FELT INDOORS, ESPECIALLY UPSTAIRS. PARKED CARS MAY SWAY.

5. MANY WAKENED. PLASTER CRACKS.

6. MANY RUN OUTSIDE. MOVING FURNITURE. CHURCH BELLS RING.

9. CRACKS IN ROADS.

10. LANDSLIDES. RIVERS OVERFLOW.

12. DEVASTATION. GROUND WAVES LIKE THE SEA.

True or false?
Soldiers marching in step can topple a bridge.

Answer: **True**

Soldiers break step when crossing small bridges. If they marched in step, the bridge might bounce and break! Many bridges shake, topple, and break under a quake's pressure.

SEARCH & FIND

Can you find four dogs?

FIND & SEARCH

I didn't know that

quakes topple bridges.

When a big quake struck Northridge, California, in 1994 three roads were closed as ten supporting bridges collapsed. The quake measured between VIII (eight) and IX (nine) on the Mercalli scale.

Quakes that hit cities cause most damage, as expensive bridges, roads, and buildings must be rebuilt. In 1995 a quake shifted the city of Kobe in Japan 5.6 feet. Two thousand feet of highway toppled sideways.

The Northridge quake was the costliest U.S. natural disaster ever.

The Kobe quake toppled a fish-shaped restaurant.

A powerful earthquake can twist solid metal train tracks as if they were pipe cleaners. This happened in Kobe, Japan, in 1995.

SEARCH & FIND ★ FIND & SEARCH
Can you find the missing road section?

SEARCH & FIND & SEARCH & FIND & SEARCH & FIND & SEARCH

Can you find the stretcher-bearers?

To see how quakes affect swampy land, fill one deep tray with dry sand and another with wet sand. Place a "building" in each tray. Bang on the table. The building in the wet sand will sink farther.

A 1985 quake had its epicenter in Michoacán, Mexico, where the ground is rock solid. I didn't know that houses can sink. The quake in Michoacán caused more damage 236 miles away in Mexico City than it did on the rocky land of Michoacán.

In 1989, wooden buildings in San Francisco slipped off their foundations and sank during an earthquake. The ground beneath them was not very solid.

Mexico City is built on a dried-up, swampy lake.

True or false?
Before a quake,
ponds get extra smelly.

Answer: **True**

As the pressure under the ground
builds up, gases build up too and leak
into groundwater, which is the water
just below land level, and pond water.
Some of these gases smell.

Animals can become
jumpy just before
a quake. It's as
if they know
what is about
to happen.

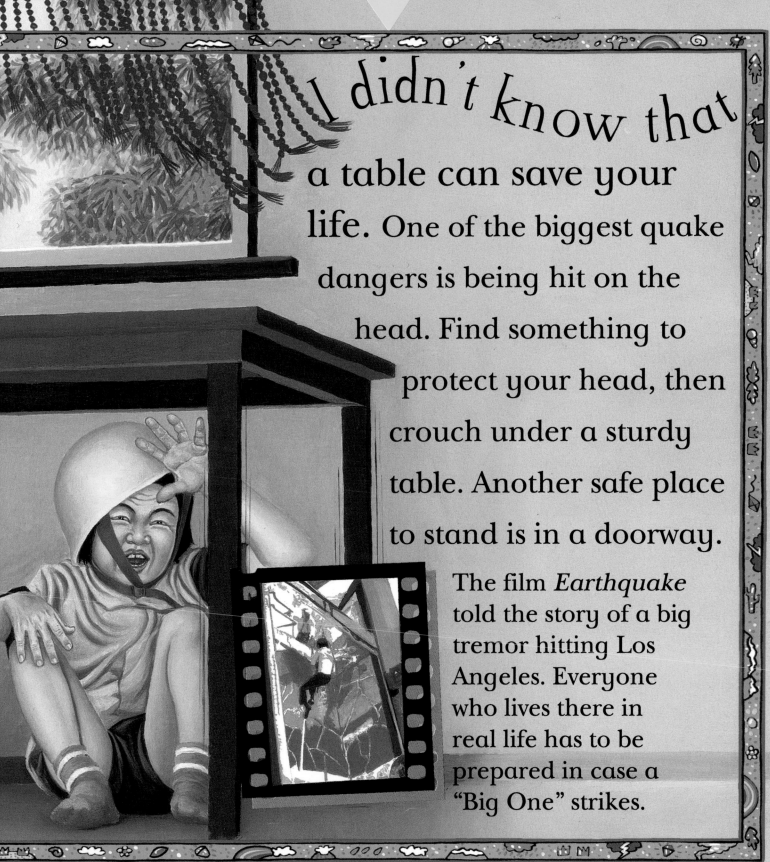

I didn't know that

a table can save your life. One of the biggest quake dangers is being hit on the head. Find something to protect your head, then crouch under a sturdy table. Another safe place to stand is in a doorway.

The film *Earthquake* told the story of a big tremor hitting Los Angeles. Everyone who lives there in real life has to be prepared in case a "Big One" strikes.

Gases in the ground often make quake fires so hot they can melt glass.

In 1970 an earthquake caused one of the worst landslides ever. The shock waves dislodged ice on the Andes, which turned into a *mudflow* that swept away the town of Yungay, Peru, killing 50,000.

SEARCH & FIND
Can you find three rooftops?
FIND & SEARCH

The Yungay landslide was 260 feet high.

 True or false?
Earthquakes make mud boil.

Answer: **True**
A quake's shock waves can make mud spurt up in 12-inch cones, or sand boils.

you can drown in mud. Sometimes, the aftereffects of an earthquake are more dangerous than the quake itself. When a quake shakes ice from mountain peaks, the ice melts and runs downward. As it flows it gathers pieces of earth and rock. The mudflow can move fast enough to sweep away people, cars, and houses.

I didn't know that

waves wash away cities. When an earthquake strikes at sea, the trembling seabed churns up monster waves. In 1755 a quake 200 miles out to sea from Lisbon, Portugal, created a huge tidal wave that destroyed the city's buildings.

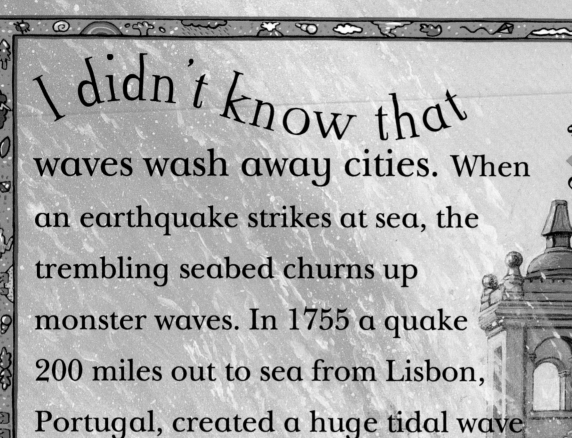

SEARCH & FIND
Can you find the donkey?

True or false?
A tidal wave is called a *tsunami.*

Answer: **True**
"Tsunami" is the proper word to use. It's a Japanese word that means "harbor wave." Japan gets hit by many tsunamis from the Pacific.

74

In 1992 an earthquake rumbled out at sea off the coast of Nicaragua, Central America. The quake made 50-foot-high waves — over ten times as tall as you — and wrecked 190 miles of coast.

True or false?
Eight elephants hold up the world.

Answer: **True**

True, if you believe the ancient Hindu myth that the earth rests on eight elephants. When an elephant shakes its head, there is an earthquake.

The ancient Mongolians thought a giant frog held up the earth.

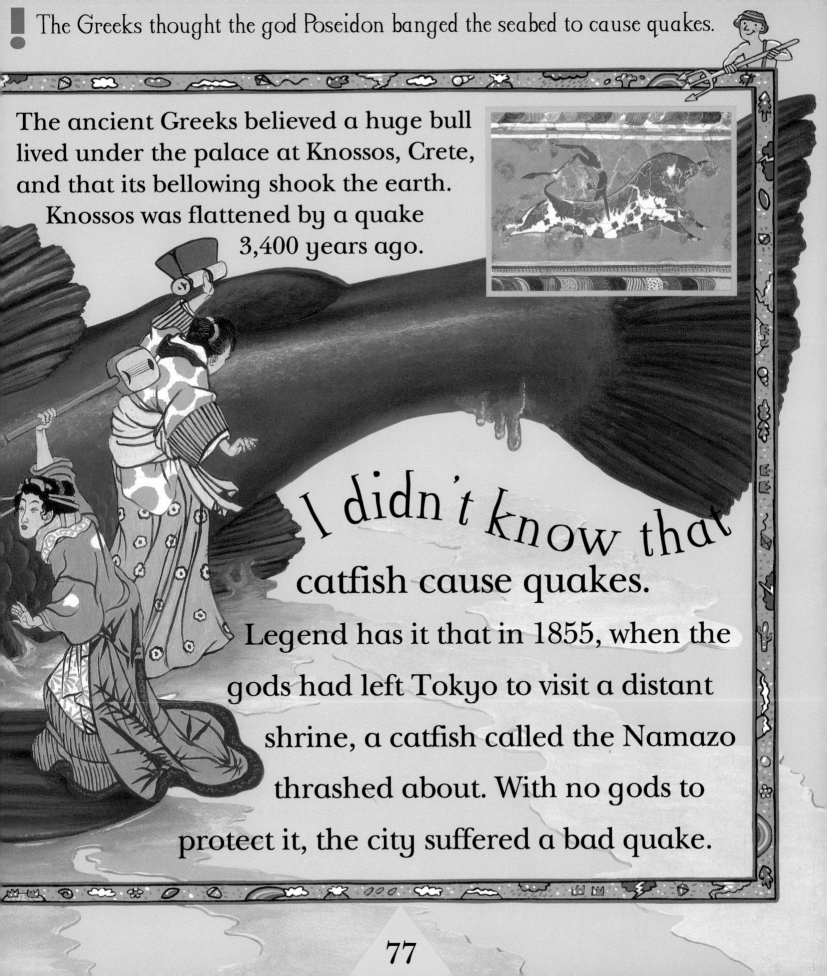

The ancient Greeks believed a huge bull lived under the palace at Knossos, Crete, and that its bellowing shook the earth. Knossos was flattened by a quake 3,400 years ago.

I didn't know that

catfish cause quakes.

Legend has it that in 1855, when the gods had left Tokyo to visit a distant shrine, a catfish called the Namazo thrashed about. With no gods to protect it, the city suffered a bad quake.

After an earthquake, rescue workers need special equipment for finding trapped victims. Infra-red cameras can "see" body heat through many layers of rubble. With the help of these, rescuers know where to start digging first.

SEARCH & FIND

Can you find three rescue dogs?

FIND SEARCH &

Japan has an annual National Disaster Prevention Day on the anniversary of the 1923 Tokyo earthquake. People practice what to do in a quake. Children wear fireproof capes (right).

I didn't know that

dogs rescue quake victims.
Sniffer dogs are used to search for victims. They are specially trained for the job. With their sensitive noses, the dogs can smell where people are lying beneath rubble.

True or false?

The worst quake this century killed 750,000 people.

Answer: **Don't know**
Some say 750,000 died at T'ang-shan, China, in 1976. But the official figure is just under 250,000.

People who flock to see an earthquake are called "disaster tourists."

Houses were made of paper.

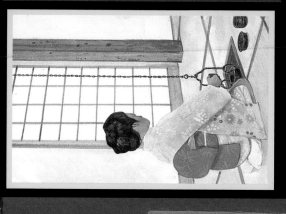

Answer: True
In Japan some houses were built of paper and balsa wood: easy and cheap to rebuild!

I didn't know that

pyramid-shaped buildings are very strong. The San Francisco Transamerica Building is wider at the bottom than at the top, and so has a sturdier base to withstand tremors.

Use building blocks to test how sturdy different shapes are when you make the table shake. A shape that is wider at the top than at the bottom is the most unstable.

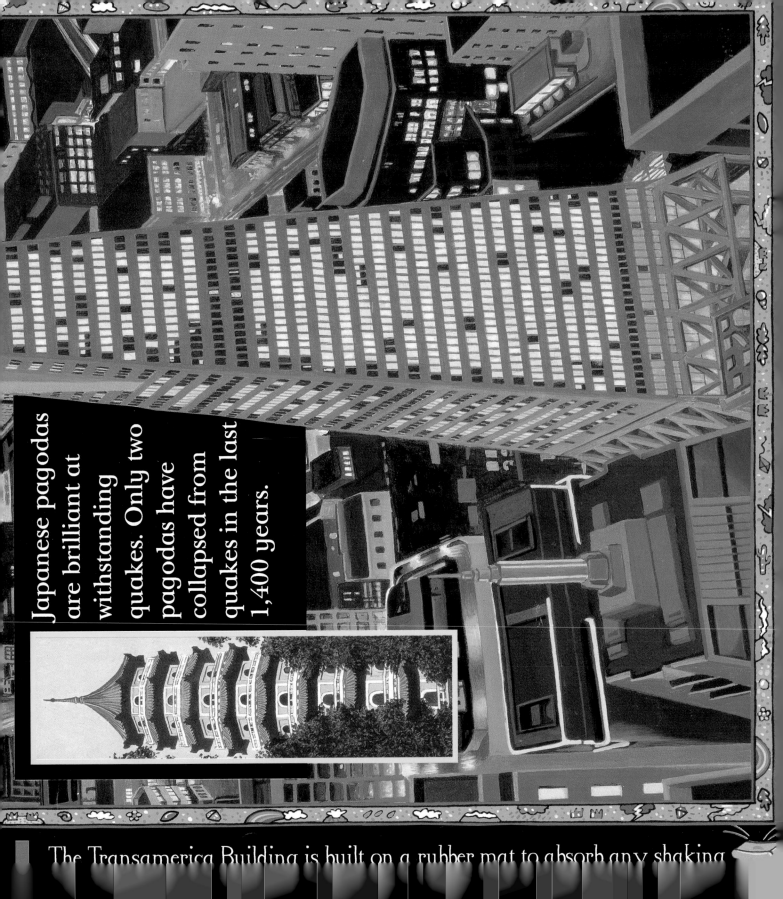

Japanese pagodas are brilliant at withstanding quakes. Only two pagodas have collapsed from quakes in the last 1,400 years.

The Transamerica Building is built on a rubber mat to absorb any shaking.

Chapter Four

tidal waves

By Kate Petty
Illustrated by
Peter Roberts
and Jo Moore

Introduction

Discover for yourself the most amazing facts about tidal waves; how they start, the power they generate and the havoc they cause.

Did you know that a tidal wave can be as tall as a skyscraper? ... that volcanoes can set off tsunamis? ... that the sea stays still as the waves move forward? ... that the moon can move water? ... that waves can break a ship in two? ... that a storm at sea can come ashore? ... that a tsunami can destroy a whole village? ... that some boats are unsinkable? ... that people fight back against waves?

True or false?

A tidal wave is caused by high tides.

Answer: **False**

Usually an earthquake or volcano is the cause of a tidal wave. Despite its name, a tidal wave has nothing to do with tides.

I didn't know that

tidal waves can be as tall as a skyscraper. A 53-foot-high tidal wave swamped the people of Lisbon, Portugal, as they fled from falling, burning buildings in the earthquake of 1755, which killed 60,000 people.

When an underwater earthquake cracks the seabed, huge pressure pushes the water above into waves. At sea the waves are far apart, but they get closer and higher as they reach the shore.

The ancient Greek philosopher Plato described a perfect city called Atlantis that disappeared under the Mediterranean Sea. It might have been engulfed by a tidal wave, or it might have simply slipped into the sea.

The biggest tidal wave ever was 295 feet, taller than a skyscraper!

I didn't know that

volcanoes can set off tsunamis.

When Krakatoa in Indonesia blew its top in 1883 the explosion was heard 3,107 miles away. The volcano caused tsunamis that killed 37,000 people on the nearby islands of Java and Sumatra.

 True or false?

There are more than 10,000 volcanoes under the Pacific Ocean.

Answer: **True**
Part of the Pacific Ocean is called the "Ring of Fire" because it has thousands of underwater volcanoes (left) and 90% of tsunamis occur here.

The eruption of Krakatoa in Indonesia could be heard in Australia.

Tsunamis are not only set off by volcanoes, they can also be set off by earthquakes. The waves can be hundreds of feet high.

Where plates pull apart magma rises and forms an ocean ridge.

Volcanoes form where two ocean plates meet.

The earth's crust is covered in plates. Where two ocean plates meet, one is forced down into the heat of the earth's mantle and may melt into magma, which can erupt as a volcano.

Surfers need good balance and coordination. They paddle out to sea and wait for a big wave to carry them to the shore. Then they stand up on the board and ride in across the face of the wave.

Crest

Trough

Circular motion of water particles

Water particles in a wave travel around in circles like rollers under a conveyor-belt. They travel up and over with the movement of the wave but down and back as the wave passes on.

I didn't know that

the sea stays still as the waves move forward. The water in a wave moves in circles. The wave is pushed forward by the wind and the movement of the water within it, but the sea itself stays in the same place.

SEARCH & FIND

FIND & SEARCH

Can you find three surfers?

Strong winds blow for great distances over the open sea, causing *swells* that can travel for thousands of miles. The rough seas seem to appear from nowhere – "out of the blue."

The highest wave ever ridden was almost 64 feet high.

I didn't know that

the moon moves water because it causes tides. Tides happen because the *gravity* of the sun and the moon pull on the earth's oceans, causing the water to rise and fall as the world spins.

This coast road in Holland is built on land that was once under the sea. High *dikes* hold back the sea.

Extra high "spring" tides occur when the sun and the moon are in line and both pulling in the same direction. Lower "neap" tides occur when the sun and moon are pulling in different directions.

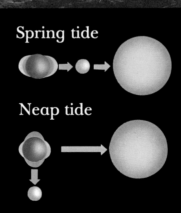

Spring tide

Neap tide

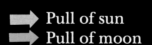

➡ Pull of sun
➡ Pull of moon

A Dutch story tells of a boy who plugged a hole in a dike with his finger.

The River Thames is affected by the tides. The Thames Barrier at Woolwich was built to protect London from flooding during exceptionally high tides.

Can you find four lit houses?

I didn't know that

waves can break a ship in two. Tropical storms at sea can strike suddenly with mountainous waves. Old wooden ships stood little chance, but even modern boats can be wrecked in stormy seas.

One of the most dangerous places in the world is Cape Horn at the very tip of South America. Sailors have always feared the dangerous conditions and the icy waters there.

A ship's computerized weather maps predict stormy weather which occurs when a warm front (round symbols) meets a cold front (triangles.)

Lighthouses warn sailors away from rocky shores at night. Make your own lighthouse from a cardboard tube. Cut out windows and paint it with stripes. Stand a flashlight inside and put a cardboard lid on top. Complete the scene with a papier mâché rock and modeling clay boats.

Cape Horn has more shipwrecks than anywhere else.

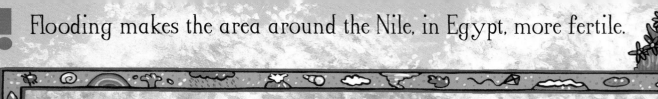

I didn't know that

a storm at sea can come ashore. Huge waves whipped up by a hurricane at sea can come ashore ahead of the storm itself. Ships end up stranded hundreds of yards from the coastline.

Hurricane

Storm surge

 True or false?
Hurricane and typhoon are both names for tropical storms.

Answer: **True**
Hurricane comes from the Carib word *huracan*, meaning "evil spirit." Typhoon comes from the Chinese *tai fung*, meaning "big wind."

When huge waves come ashore ahead of the storm it is called a storm surge.

A storm surge can raise the level of the sea by 20 feet. Flooding after a tropical storm in Bangladesh in 1991 killed 250,000 people and left millions without their homes, animals, or possessions.

A hurricane can move at the speed of a car down a highway.

I didn't know that

a tsunami could destroy a whole village. In 1992, two thousand villagers were killed when a tsunami, 85 feet high, crashed into their fragile wooden homes in Flores, Indonesia, causing devastation.

 True or false?
People at sea don't notice tsunamis.

Answer: **True**

In 1896, Japanese fishermen had no idea that one of the waves beneath their boats went on to kill 27,000 people back home.

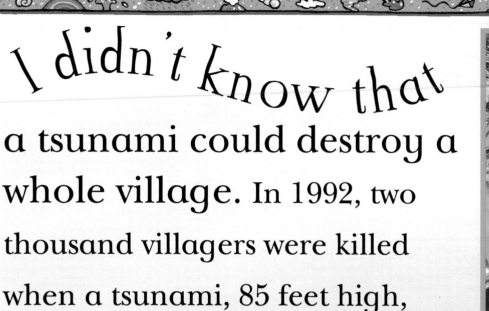

In 1998, islanders settling down for the evening in Papua New Guinea were caught off-guard by three 49-foot tsunamis, set off by an earthquake 12 miles out to sea. More than 2,000 people died. These survivors came back to find their homes had been devastated.

In 1960, a tsunami in Chile killed more than 1,000 people and destroyed 50,000 homes. Fourteen hours later it slammed into Hilo, Hawaii, killing an additional 61 people.

Alaska

Hawaii

Isla de Chiloe
Chile

A tsunami can move as fast as a jet airplane.

1,517 people died when the liner *Titanic* sank in 1912.

True or false?
Sailors have been known to survive for several days after capsizing in cold waters.

Answer: **True**
In January 1997 around-the-world yachtsman Tony Bullimore spent five days under his overturned 60–foot yacht before being rescued 1,300 miles south of Australia.

Helicopters are useful in sea rescues because they can hover while a survivor is winched to safety. They use radar and infra-red scanners to pinpoint people in the sea.

The sea can be a dangerous place. Wearing a life jacket could save your life. Never go sailing without telling someone where you are going and when you expect to be back.

I didn't know that

some boats are unsinkable.
Modern lifeboats have the power to
skim over the tops of very high
waves. They are also designed to
right themselves if they keel over.
Satellite links help them to locate
a ship in trouble.

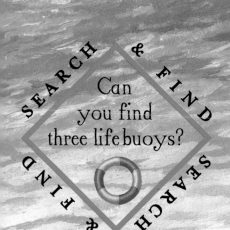

SEARCH ✦ FIND
Can
you find
three life buoys?
FIND ✦ SEARCH

Two fishermen were adrift for 177 days after a cyclone hit.

Families who live in tsunami areas need an *evacuation* plan and an emergency kit on hand. The kit should contain: a flashlight and extra batteries, a portable battery radio, a first-aid kit with medicines, emergency food and water, a canopener, money, and sturdy shoes.

Eye-witnesses to tsunamis describe the way the sea first pulls back with a hissing, sucking sound, rather like the noise of a jet engine, before it rears up in a huge, engulfing wave. The rumble of a nearby earthquake is another warning sign.

! Tsunamis can be caused by meteorites landing in the sea.

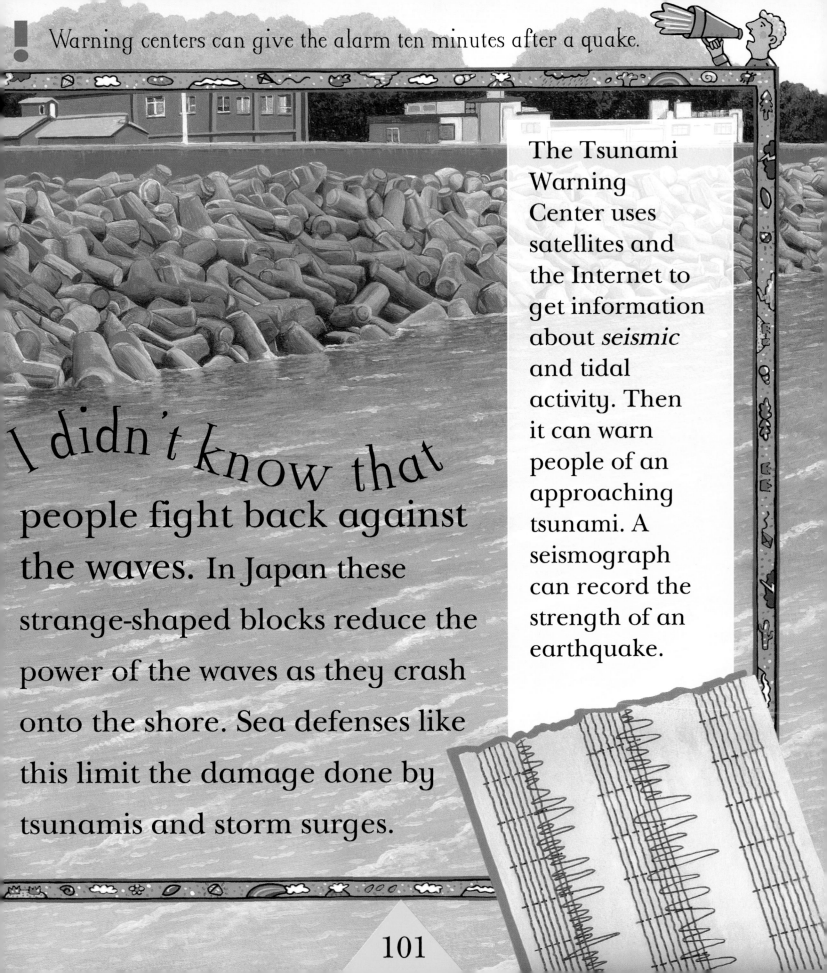

The Tsunami Warning Center uses satellites and the Internet to get information about *seismic* and tidal activity. Then it can warn people of an approaching tsunami. A seismograph can record the strength of an earthquake.

I didn't know that people fight back against the waves. In Japan these strange-shaped blocks reduce the power of the waves as they crash onto the shore. Sea defenses like this limit the damage done by tsunamis and storm surges.

"St. Elmo's fire" can sometimes be seen around the mast of a ship in stormy seas. It occurs when the moving air inside a storm cloud builds up static electricity which gathers around the highest point of the ship, the mast.

Waterspouts are an awe-inspiring sight, but fortunately they are rarely dangerous. They usually last about 15 minutes. Most waterspouts are only 15 to 30 feet thick and between 165 and 330 feet high.

I didn't know that

the sea can be sucked up into the sky. A waterspout is a tornado at sea. When rapidly rising warm air meets falling cool air, it sets up a spinning funnel, which sucks up the water from the surface of the sea.

 True or false?
Sometimes one waterspout can follow after another.

Answer: **True**
At Martha's Vineyard (off the southeast coast of Massachusetts) in 1896, there were three waterspouts within just 45 minutes.

In 1958, sailors in the Adriatic Sea saw five waterspouts at once.

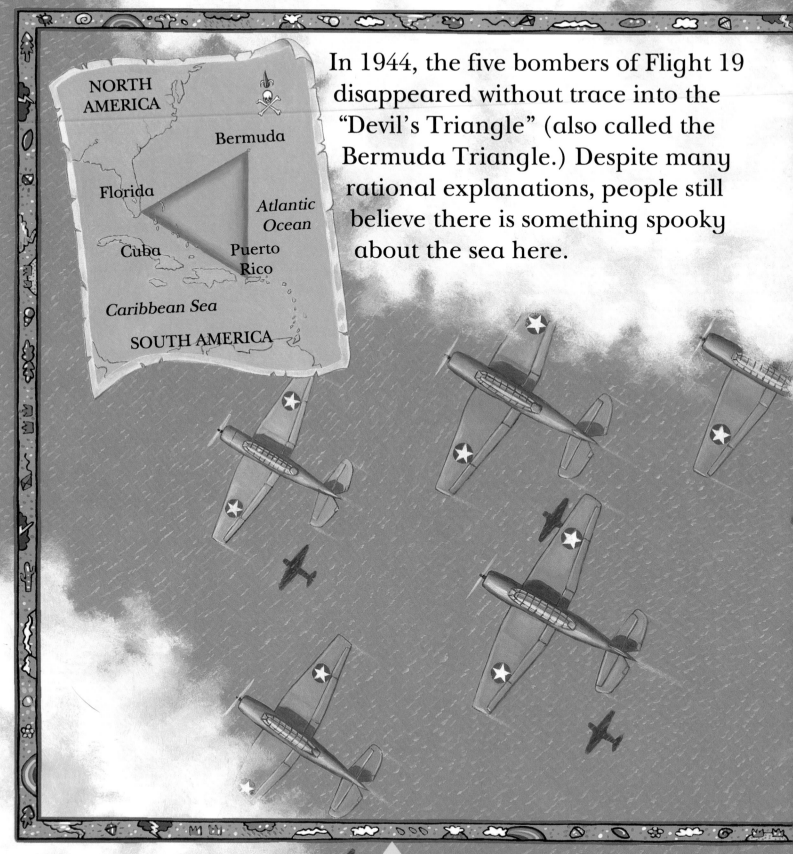

NORTH AMERICA

Bermuda

Florida

Atlantic Ocean

Cuba

Puerto Rico

Caribbean Sea

SOUTH AMERICA

In 1944, the five bombers of Flight 19 disappeared without trace into the "Devil's Triangle" (also called the Bermuda Triangle.) Despite many rational explanations, people still believe there is something spooky about the sea here.

I didn't know that

there are still unsolved mysteries of the sea. More than 70 ships and 20 planes have been lost in the "Bermuda Triangle," maybe because this stormy area of the Atlantic Ocean has undersea earthquakes and volcanoes as well as awkward *currents*.

"El Niño" is the movement of warm water in the Pacific, eastward from Indonesia toward the Americas.

America

Warm water

True or false?

El Niño can cause flooding in the desert.

Answer: **True**

In 1983, El Niño brought high winds and flooding to the Arizona desert. It can cause strange weather, like snow in places that are usually hot or drought in wet places. It can also often bring violent weather.

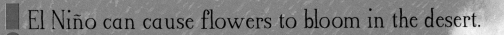
El Niño can cause flowers to bloom in the desert.

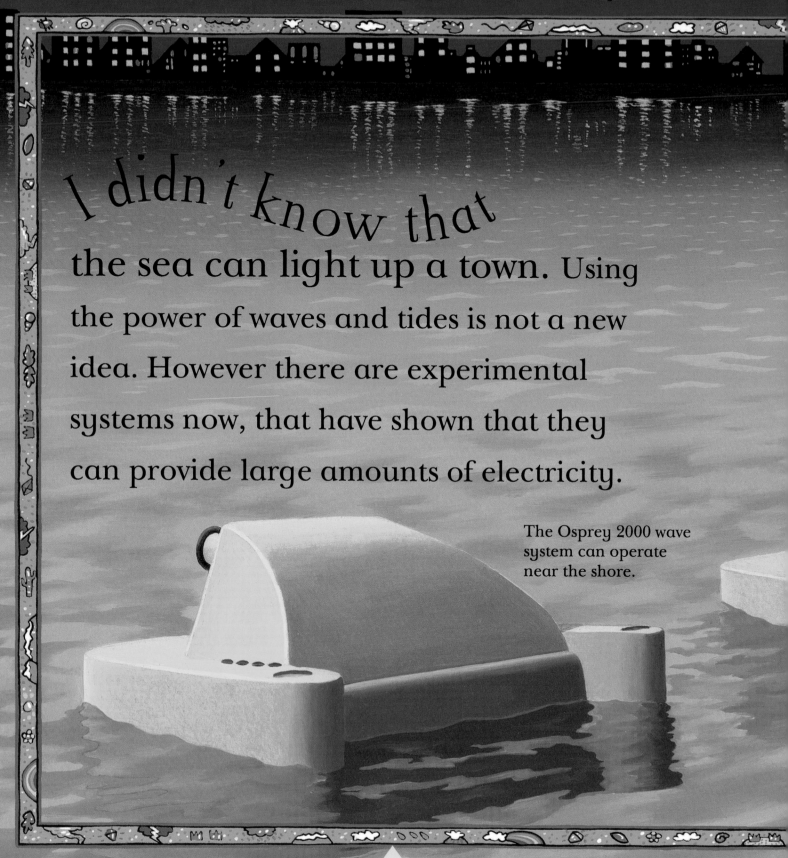

I didn't know that

the sea can light up a town. Using the power of waves and tides is not a new idea. However there are experimental systems now, that have shown that they can provide large amounts of electricity.

The Osprey 2000 wave system can operate near the shore.

Run a faucet over a toy waterwheel and see how the power of the water turns the wheel. The turning of the wheel produces energy. You can make a waterwheel with a spool that can spin on a pencil.

Wave power is a way of generating electricity. One day it should be possible to harness the power of strong, deep water waves out at sea.

The biggest waterpower plant is ITAIPU. Built by Brazil and Paraguay, it supplies a quarter of Brazil's electricity and more than three quarters of Paraguay's.

Tide-powered water mills have been used for thousands of years.

Glossary

Air pressure

The weight of the air pressing down on the land. High pressure usually means good weather and low pressure means bad.

Beaufort scale

An illustrated scale measuring wind force from calm to hurricane.

Black smoker

A hot spring on the ocean floor.

Caldera

A huge volcanic crater, formed when the slopes of a volcano collapse into the empty magma chamber.

Climate

The sort of weather a particular place has come to expect over a long time.

Condensation

This happens when a gas, such as water vapor, cools to form droplets of liquid. Clouds are formed this way with droplets of water.

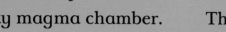

Cone

The "mountain" of hardened lava that builds up around a volcano.

Core

The center of the earth.

Crater

The bowl-shaped hollow at the top of a volcano, above the vent.

Creepmeter

A machine that measures "creep," that is, how far the earth's plates move.

Crust

The outer layer of the earth.

Currents

Movement of water in the oceans set up by the winds and the spin of the world.

Dike

A wall that holds back water.

Dormant

A volcano is dormant, or sleeping, between eruptions.

Epicenter

The center of an earthquake on the ground.

Fault lines

Cracks in the earth's crust.

Erupt

When a volcano erupts it throws out gases, rocks, and ash onto the earth's surface.

Focus

The starting point of an earthquake underground.

Magma

Hot molten rock that is still below the earth's surface.

Evacuation

Clearing people from a building or place which is dangerous.

Gravity

A force that "pulls" objects toward each other, like a falling apple is pulled toward the ground.

Mantle

The hot layer of the earth between the crust and the core.

Mercalli scale

A range of numbers that describes the power of an earthquake, based on what

Evaporation

This happens when a liquid, such as water, is heated and turns into a gas that rises into the air.

Infra-red

Satellites can use infra-red rays to show different heat patterns as pictures.

witnesses of the quake saw.

Extinct

A volcano is extinct when it will never erupt again.

Lava

Magma that has reached the earth's surface. It cools as flows on land or pillows under the sea.

Meteorite

Space rock that has broken away from a comet's fiery tail and smashes into a planet or moon.

Monsoon
The name of the south-westerly wind that brings heavy rain to parts of Asia in the summer; also the name given to the rainy season in those places.

Mudflow
A "river" of rock, earth, and water that can start out when an ice-covered mountain peak is shaken and melted in a quake.

Plates
Large sections of the earth's crust that move constantly against each other.

Seismic
To do with earthquakes (seism is another word for earthquake).

Seismograph
A machine that measures the force of an earthquake. A printout from the machine is called a seismogram.

Static electricity
Electricity that isn't flowing in a current. It builds up from friction (such as when

you rub a balloon or stroke a cat), or from lots of activity in a cloud.

Storm surge
Waves blown before the wind that can cause flooding, especially if forced through a narrow channel.

Swell
The rise and fall of the waves on the open sea.

Tropical storms
Violent storms that develop in the hot (over 80° F), moist air above warm seas near the Equator in summer and fall.

Tsunami
A giant wave, caused by a volcanic eruption or an earthquake.

Volcanologist
Someone who studies volcanoes.

Index

Index